Cover Design by Tenesha L. Curtis

Tenesha L. Curtis, Managing Editor
A.E. Williams, Developmental Editor
Nafari Vanaski, Copyeditor
Marie Patrick, Proofreader

THE POLICE ENCOUNTER BIBLE

Tommy Bridgeman

Contents

Introduction

The extensive research, time, and media attention dedicated to the art of policing within Black America influenced me to highlight the importance of this issue. As a pastor and teacher of an African American congregation and a servant to my community, the Black community, I felt that there could never be too many voices or perspectives on the aforementioned subject. In graduate school, I was assigned to find a subject to research and present my findings to the class, then prepare to defend my position on the subject when my professor, Dr. Charles Thomas, and my classmates challenged me on the facts as well as my perspective.

The topic that I chose was the problem with police "policing" the police. My initial argument was that there was no way that there could be any real justice for those who may be victimized by law enforcement officers when it was the police who policed themselves. For this very reason, many times, when an officer is accused of a crime or misdoing, he or she is not prosecuted or held accountable for the act. As I continued my research, I discovered that so many of the suspicions that myself and many other Americans were concerned about regarding policing in America were true. And, in many ways, worse than we could have ever imagined.

I become consumed by the subject. Other than my study and research for the necessary courses to complete my Master of Divinity degree, no subject had ever had this impact on my life, even though I had read many stories and headlines. I sought to answer every question that came to my mind on the subject as well as being prepared for the questions that might be asked by my classmates and Dr. Thomas. My research led me to the internet where I had the ability to watch video footage of police encounters all over the country and even many abroad. I spent countless hours watching videos from the beginning to the end, logging the nature of the encounter, listening intently to the officer's questions, examining every response by civilians and how the situation would unfold. There were times that I was in my office moments before having to go into the sanctuary of the church to preach that I found myself watching and studying a recording. I began to recognize the patterns of police encounters.

After watching hundreds, perhaps thousands, of live, uncut, raw contacts, I could often predict what the officers would say and sometimes what they would do. The thing that really caught my attention and probably was the greatest motivation in writing this book and teaching the seminar "Think Free, Feel Free, Live Free" was the fact that many encounters involved everyday law-abiding citizens just like me—people walking home from work committing no crime, kids walking to or from a playground, a call from a "concerned" citizen or even people taking pictures in public. The footage painted a picture for me. It showed me that anyone at any time could find themselves in an encounter with a police officer and could have their rights violated or worse. Law enforcement contact has the potential to leave a civilian with his or her dignity ripped apart. Having had this happen to me in the past, I was familiar with how helpless and hopeless one can feel during and after experiences with the police. After I made my presentation to my class and successfully defended my opposition to police policing the police, Dr. Thomas suggested that I continue to develop this work.

The purpose of writing this book is to teach people what I have learned and prayerfully equip them with information that will educate them on their rights, as well as how to assert them during an encounter. Given the seriousness of police encounters and understanding the fact that some officers will violate your rights, hurt you or even kill you, the reader will learn from this book a strategy for telling your story of what happened during this encounter in a way that does not rely solely on a police report that might be fabricated. Often, everyday citizens find themselves in court defending against charges that are false. By following a few basic steps, known as "The 3 C's," from this book, the story of your police encounter is recorded and can be told by yourself or others — whether you survive the interaction or not.

Chapter One
Own Your Freedom

It's important that we, as Black Americans, completely embrace our American heritage in order to claim the rights that are promised to us in the United States Constitution. While I'm naturally extremely proud and scholastically aware of my African American ancestry, it's the "American" in me that is entitled to unalienable rights and protections under the laws in the country of my citizenship.

The Declaration of Independence, primarily drafted by Thomas Jefferson, is undeniably a symbol of liberty for the United States of America. Jefferson drafted what he believed was a core set of principles that resided in the hearts of every American. It represented America's desire to be free from the control and tyranny of Great Britain. On July 4, 1776, the Continental Congress signed the Declaration of Independence, declaring the thirteen American colonies independent from Britain. These colonies became a small part of what we now know as the United States of America. [1]

Arguably, the most famous line from the Declaration, is a "truth" that all Americans must know, accept, and be willing to defend. "We hold these truths to be self-evident, that all men are created equal, that they are endowed by their Creator with certain unalienable Rights that, among them are life, Liberty, and the pursuit of happiness." This statement implies that we, as Americans, are *all* free.

On June 21, 1788, the United States Constitution was ratified after being drafted for months by James Madison after the Constitutional Convention of 1787. This U.S. Constitution was the blueprint that laid out how the United States government should operate, ultimately becoming the framework of our current system of government.

The first three articles were essential in the molding of the United States government then, and now.

The first article established what we now know as the Legislative Branch, which consists of the United States Congress, or the U.S. Senate and U.S. House of Representatives. The second article established the Executive Branch

– which establishes the President and Vice President of the United States. The third article established the Supreme Court of the United States and the court system.

In order to continue the implication of freedom expressed in the Declaration of Independence, ten amendments were added to the Constitution that became known as the Bill of Rights:

I.   Grants the right to express religion, freedom of speech, right to peacefully assemble, freedom of the press, and the right to petition the government.

II.   Grants the right to keep and bear arms (guns).

III.   Places restrictions on the quartering of soldiers in private homes.

IV.   Prohibits search and seizures of personal property and sets requirements for search warrants in regard to Probable Cause.

V.   Sets rules for trials by jury, protects the right to due process, prohibits self-incrimination, and prevents anyone from being tried for the same crime twice.

VI.   Establishes the right to a fair and speedy trial by jury as well as the rights to be notified of accusers, to confront accusers, to

obtain witnesses and to retain counsel
(lawyers).

VII.   Establishes the right to a trial by
jury in civil cases.

VIII.   Prohibits excessive fines and bails
as cruel and unusual punishment.

IX.   Protects rights not enumerated by
the Constitution.

X.   Expresses that the federal
government only has powers delegated or
enumerated by the United States Constitution.[2]

Over the last two centuries, there have
been several critical amendments made to the
United States Constitution. These amendments
were put into place in order to create even more
freedom for citizens of the United States. To
reference a few, the 13th Amendment
effectively abolished the enslavement of
Africans after the Civil War; the 15th
Amendment allowed African Americans to
vote; the 17th Amendment allowed for election
of Senators by popular vote; the 19th
Amendment allowed women to vote; and the
24th Amendment eliminated the Poll Tax and
afforded poor Americans the ability to vote.[3]

All Americans are governed by this set of
laws and are called upon to obey them. Any

deviation, abuse, or disregard for these laws could result in some form of lawful correction. This is how a civilized society maintains a system of law and order. In order for these laws to provide the protections and privileges of us all, it's important that we accept our American citizenship.

Citizenship is at the base of independence and freedoms under the law.

Although many of us are citizens by birth, others have gone through the lengthy process of becoming a legal citizen of the United States of America. Upon completion of that process, new citizens must swear an oath to the Constitution and become a full citizen with the same rights and privileges afforded to natural born citizens.

Despite all these freedoms that have been provided to citizens over hundreds of years, Black Americans must confront the tumultuous history of America and its relationship with those of African descent. Freedom is a liberty that should not be taken lightly.

As we all know, the Africans that were enslaved in America, while enduring involuntary servitude, indescribable mental and physical abuse, and inhumane living conditions, immeasurably contributed to the wealth and prosperity of this country. These are the direct ancestors of many Black American citizens today. The enslavement of Africans was a core cause of the Civil War.

The general disregard the nation seems to have for the progress struggled for by our ancestors in order to afford today's African Americans the rights they currently have is disheartening, to say the least. Black Americans have allowed themselves to be identified as "less- American" or some type of "sub-American" with fewer rights and privileges than other Americans.

Black Americans don't feel like Americans. Despite all the progress over the centuries made in the Declaration of Independence and the Bill of Rights, Black Americans are often left out of the equation. This lack of respect for the community and blatant disregard of their constitutional rights (and there are many) convince many Black Americans to deny their "American" and just consider themselves "Black." However, one doesn't lose his or her "American" simply because they refuse to accept or acknowledge their American heritage. Fully understanding and owning your "American" and all of its protections is the foundation that you must stand on, especially if you find yourself in an encounter with law enforcement.

Chapter Two
Important Terms
and Court Cases

In order for you to protect yourself during an encounter with law enforcement, it is necessary to be a well-informed citizen and confident in your constitutional rights. Knowing your rights is the beginning of claiming your freedom and learning how to respectfully assert them is the best way to protect yourself during an encounter with law enforcement. Every time you are involved in an interaction with a law enforcement officer, remember that he is sticking to a script and common practices that he knows like the back of his hand.

While we want to believe that the law and those enforcing it are always lawful, there is overwhelming evidence to argue just the opposite. Police officers are human beings, though held to a higher standard of lawfulness, and are sworn to serve and protect. We would be remiss to dismiss the fact that just like civilians, police officers are imperfect. While one in four Americans have some sort of criminal history, studies show that each year, an average of three officers are arrested every day for committing crimes. [4]

If being a law-abiding citizen decreases your chances of having frequent contact with law enforcement, being a Black American more than triples those chances. Many Black Americans are introduced to police before the age of 23 through routine traffic stops, stop-and-frisk, reasonable suspicion, trespassing, or minor infractions. Being prepared for these "random" occurrences could be the difference between a peaceful interaction or one where your rights may be violated.

Terms You Should Know

Probable Cause

Probably cause is the standard that a police officer must meet in order to have legal justification, to make and arrest, obtain a warrant, or search a person or his property. Probable Cause is also the standard by which grand juries issue criminal indictments. [5]

Probable Cause was introduced in the Fourth Amendment which states, *The right of the people to be secure in their persons, houses, papers, and effects, against unreasonable searches and seizures, shall not be violated, and no warrants shall issue, but upon probable cause, supported by Oath or affirmation, and particularly describing the place to be searched and the persons or things to be seized."*

Probable Cause can be established in certain situations:

- An officer has a desire or a warrant to arrest you.
- An officer witnesses you committing an illegal act such as theft, assault, DUI, etc.

Many times, the only charge that one faces after an unwarranted arrest or detainment is *resisting arrest*. Often, when an officer steps outside of his legal boundaries and recklessly violates a citizen's rights by illegally searching their person, property, home or vehicle, by illegally detaining, or by physically assaulting them, the more difficult it becomes for that officer to establish probable cause. This can cause them to further violate your rights in order to create a narrative that may benefit them. For example, an officer may put you into cuffs as if you're under arrest, which may get a rise out of a citizen who is within their legal rights or has not broken any articulable laws. Without any probable cause, it's difficult for them to justify any act of enforcement. Believing that you have done nothing wrong, the average law-abiding citizen, who may not be used to being treated like a criminal, may tense up in objection to being handcuffed or maybe even verbally object. If the officer's intentions are to arrest you right then, at that moment, accept that this is the case, and DO NOT RESIST! Resisting arrest is a crime and you can be charged for it, whether you're guilty or not.

Reasonable Articulable Suspicion

Reasonable Articulable Suspicion is a standard used in criminal procedure used to determine the legality of a police officer to approach a civilian. Reasonable articulable suspicion needs to be established before an officer can detain you, search you, or prevent you from leaving an encounter. The officer must be able to demonstrate at least one of the following:

- That you're about to commit a crime.
- That you're in the act of committing a crime
- That you've just committed a crime.

Reasonable articulable suspicion has to be established in order for the detainment to be legal and lawful.

If an officer gets a call that a suspect wearing a black jacket, blue jeans, and a red cap has just assaulted someone at the neighborhood store, and you, a lawful citizen, happen to be in the same neighborhood wearing a black jacket, blue jeans, and the telling red cap, this could be seen as reasonable articulable suspicion for an officer to approach or stop you. Because you are unaware of any crime or 911 call, there naturally may be a level of shock and uncertainty upon being approached by police under such circumstances.

In any encounter, no matter the severity of the situation or the demeanor or tactics of law enforcement, REMAIN CALM. You are a free law-abiding citizen who has rights to protect you. Remaining calm and confident in those rights and freedoms can save your life! Therefore, it is key to remember that you are under no legal obligation to talk to police at any time, or present them with identification unless you have been lawfully placed under arrest.

An officer can claim that he is "suspicious" of you for one reason or another, but "appearing suspicious" solely is not a crime and cannot be used as *reasonable articulable suspicion* to force you to identify yourself. Offering a reasonable explanation for your presence in the area in question should satisfy their suspicion. If your explanation is not sufficient for them, the officer may still ask for your identification, "just to run your name" or check for warrants. However, by now, you have already addressed their suspicion and you are under no legal obligation to identify yourself.

There are, however, some states that are known as "Stop and Identify" states. In these states an officer can detain you without arrest and you would be required by law to present them with identification or your legal name and date of birth.

If you are pulled over by law enforcement while operating a vehicle, you are required by law to present your driver's license, registration, and in most states, proof of insurance. Whether you believe the stop is valid or not doesn't matter. Complying with identifying yourself and your vehicle is essential in covering yourself and will hopefully set a "lawful" tone for the remainder of the interaction. An internet search will inform you of your state's Stop and Identify laws.

Trespassing

In order for you to be guilty of trespassing, there needs to be a visible "No Trespassing" sign posted. Not seeing the sign will not prevent you from being charged with trespassing. You must be "physically present" on the property. If you have been asked to leave by a business owner, property manager, a private homeowner or lessee, and if you do not, then they are within their rights to call law enforcement and have you removed from the property.

For example, you might be walking through a parking lot that you believe is a shortcut to your favorite corner store and there are no trespassing signs posted. If the store manager asks you to leave and calls law enforcement, a police officer cannot legally charge you with trespassing, nor can he legally detain you if you have not previously been removed from that property for trespassing. A police officer cannot be the complainant unless the property is his personal property.

Obstruction

If you are approached by law enforcement and the interaction leads to detainment or arrest that you believe to be unlawful, you have rights. Assert them. In doing so, you may be hit with another term you should become familiar with, as it is commonly used by law enforcement when they may be violating a citizen's rights – obstruction. Obstruction of justice is a broad term, which implies one is preventing an officer from doing his job or from completing an investigation.

Often, you will hear the terms *interfering* and *hindering* if you intend to stand up for your rights, ask questions, or challenge the legality of the interaction. These terms are generally used in an attempt to intimidate you into giving up your rights and complying with the officer's every command, even if unlawful. There are three elements that must be met for an individual to be guilty of obstruction of justice:

1.   **An obstructive act** such as lying to an officer, physically restraining or impeding an officer from conducting an arrest, or preventing the officer from performing their legal and lawful duty.

2.   **An intentional and deliberate act** to obstruct the officer's ability to do his job such as misleading, hindering, or prohibiting the officer's ability to investigate a crime or make an arrest.

3.   **A deliberate, criminal intent to obstruct** the officer from arresting a person who has committed a crime and is being lawfully arrested. This also includes assisting a suspect in his or her attempt to flee or avoid arrest or conviction.

Officers will accuse you of obstructing justice if you are not willing to identify yourself or cooperate. At the root of obstruction of justice is a crime or an offense. If you're stopped on the street, and you haven't committed a crime, and the officer does not have probable cause to arrest you or reasonable articulable suspicion to detain you, a refusal to speak to the officer or to identify yourself is *not* an obstruction of justice. Check your state's Stop and Identify statutes.

If you do not live in a Stop and Identify state, it will be difficult to make a charge of obstruction of justice stick. You *can* refuse to identify yourself if you're not lawfully under arrest.

Failure to Provide Identification

A charge of Failure to Provide Identification can only occur if you have been lawfully arrested and are being processed into jail, or you are lawfully stopped by a law enforcement officer in a Stop and Identify state and refuse to produce identification. While this is a legal charge, it cannot be lawfully enforced without a crime having been committed.

The Supreme Court has ruled that someone being asked to identify themselves without probable cause to arrest them and book them into a local jail is a violation of their Fourth Amendment rights. The Fourth Amendment of The U.S. Constitution *protects personal privacy, and every citizen's right to be free from unreasonable government intrusion*

*into their persons, homes, businesses, and
property -- whether through police stops of
citizens on the street, arrests, or searches of
homes and businesses.*

The founders believed that this is a
privilege that we enjoy as free people in
America. That freedom also affords you the
opportunity to freely give your identification if
you so choose.

Important Cases and Rulings

ESCOBEDO v. ILLINOIS (1964)

When Danny Escobedo was arrested and
taken in for questioning, he was refused the
counsel of an attorney and subsequently
confessed to murder. Escobedo was convicted
of murder. The confession was later deemed
inadmissible as it was elicited after he had been
denied the assistance of counsel.

The Supreme Court ruled that
Escobedo's Sixth Amendment rights had been
violated. Any statement that had been made
from the moment he had been denied an
opportunity to seek legal counsel could not be
used against him in a criminal trial.

MIRANDA v. ARIZONA (1966)

Ernesto Miranda was arrested at his home in connection to a kidnapping and rape. He was brought into interrogation by police officers who then obtained a written confession within two hours. At Miranda's defense, his attorney requested that the confession be ruled admissible into the court as Miranda told by officers of his right to have an attorney present during interrogation.

The state of Arizona held that Miranda's constitutional rights had not been violated, so the case was brought to the Supreme Court. The Supreme Court ruled in a majority that

Miranda's Fifth Amendment rights had been violated. The court also ruled that defendants must be made aware of these rights in order to voluntarily waive such rights if they desire.

This case is the reason that officers must read you your rights at the time of arrest. This is why these rights are known as the "Miranda Rights" or the "Miranda Warning". At the time of arrest, officers are required to inform you of the following rights (phrasing varies):

- You have the right to remain silent. Anything you say can and will be used against you in court.
- You have the right to consult an attorney before answering any questions.
- You have the right to have an attorney present during questioning.
- If you cannot afford an attorney, one will be appointed for you.
- You have the right to stop answering at any time.

TERRY v. OHIO (1968)

Officer McFadden observed two men outside of a store walking up to the window, then away, several times. A third man met up with the pair and engaged in conversation. The plain- clothed officer suspected that the men were planning to rob the store. McFadden approached the men and, after identifying himself as an officer, asked what they were doing. The men mumbled back a response. McFadden then grabbed Terry, turned him around, and patted him down to determine if he was armed. The search revealed a gun in Terry's coat pocket. After conducting the same search on the second man, another gun was revealed. Once at trial, the officer testified that he thought the men may have been armed. Terry was convicted of carrying a concealed weapon in a trial by jury. Terry appealed to the Supreme Court.

The Supreme Court ruled in a majority that officers may conduct a search limited for weapons when they observe unusual conduct leading them to reasonably suspect criminal activity is afoot, and the individuals involved are armed. Terry v. Ohio popularized the "Terry Stop" which established the constitutionality of a limited search for weapons when an officer has reasonable suspicion to believe a crime is afoot based on the circumstances.

A limited search of the outside of your body consists only of a pat down for weapons. This is done for officer and citizen safety. If an officer asks if he can pat you down, be sure to verbalize that you do not consent to a search of your person, property, or documents. In order to enter into your pockets, purses, bags, briefcases, and other personal effects, the officer requires consent, or a warrant signed by a judge. Often citizens make the mistake of answering questions from the officer during a pat down regarding the contents of their pockets. The law only gives the officer the right to pat you down for weapons. If the pat down does not produce a weapon, you are under no legal obligation to answer questions about the content of your pockets.

FRAZIER v. CUPP (1969)

Acting on a tip, police picked up and interrogated Martin E. Frazier, a 20-year-old U.S. Marine, about his possible involvement in the murder of Russell Anton Marleau. Frazier and his cousin, Jerry Lee Rawls, were seen at a bar with the victim before the murder. They also had a gym bag in their possession that was searched by police with Rawls' consent.

During the interrogation, police falsely informed Frazier that Rawls had already confessed and implicated him in the murder. Frazier denied any involvement in the crime and suggested speaking with an attorney, but police continued to question him. Police elicited a confession, which was used against him at trial. Mr. Frazier was convicted of murder and Mr. Rawls pleaded guilty to the murder of Russell Marleau. Frazier, however, appealed his conviction to the United States Supreme Court. The Court stated the trial judge followed necessary protocol by instructing the jury to disregard the references to Rawls's statements. The Court agreed the prosecution did not emphasize Rawls's statements over other evidence and the statements alone were not "touted to the jury as a crucial part of the prosecution's case.

"The Court ruled Frazier did not formally request an attorney and that the statement, on its own, did not render the confession involuntary based on a "totality of the circumstances" view.

The Court dismissed the illegal search argument, citing consent was legally obtained from Rawls and his mother. The Court ruled Rawls, a co-owner of the gym bag, was authorized to give consent to search the bag, even though items in certain compartments of the bag belonged to Frazier.

In a nutshell, this Supreme Court ruling has essentially given officers the ability to be misleading, disingenuous, and even lie during an investigation or interrogation. It's vital for you to know your rights, how to assert them, and the laws that support them. The laws are there for our protection, and if the forefathers believed that we needed this type of protection during an encounter with law enforcement, then there must have been a good reason to institute such protections. I can't think of any reason that an American citizen would ignore such protections.

GLIK v. CUNNIFFE (2011)

When Simon Glik, a private citizen, filmed Boston, Massachusetts, police officers making an arrest in a public park, and the officers observed that Glik was recording the arrest, they arrested him and he was subsequently charged with wiretapping, disturbing the peace, and aiding in the escape of a prisoner. Glik then sued the City of Boston and the arresting officers, claiming that they violated his constitutional rights.

In a unanimous decision, the United States Court of Appeals for the First Circuit held that the officers violated Glik's constitutional rights and that the officers were not entitled to qualified immunity. The Court ruled that the right to film public officials in public places was "clearly established," and that Glik's actions did not violate state law.

However, the court also ruled that the right to film public officials was subject to reasonable limitations with respect to the time, place, and manner in which the recording was conducted.

After losing the appeal, Boston reached a settlement with Glik in which they agreed to pay him $170,000 in damages and attorney's fees. This was the first case in which a United States Circuit Court of Appeals explicitly ruled that private citizens have a right to film police officers in public spaces. The case drew media attention across the United States and was cited favorably by other United States Circuit Courts of Appeals that reached similar conclusions in other cases.

Police are subject to the same laws that govern all citizens of America. There are guidelines and policies that officers must follow, just as there are laws and rules that citizens must follow. These policies and laws, if violated, could be harmful to the reputation of our local police departments and negatively impact our criminal justice system.

If an officer violates policy or the law, it could lead to a dangerous person or persons being released from custody or freed from prison over a violation of rights. Violations like this could affect a small community's economic standings and cost the city and police department huge sums of money by settling lawsuits of citizens whose rights were violated or were subjected to some form of misconduct or abuse of power.

The law-enforcement and the civilian communities have the same problem. Both groups are judged by the actions of the worst actors in each group. It's true that officers don't know what to expect when encountering a member of the public. It could very well be a person who has a challenge in life and wants to hurt someone and the officer is doing what we pay them to do — serve and protect.

However, on the other hand, there are officers who are just as dangerous as those members of the community who want to hurt someone. Each group has the right to protect itself.

Chapter Three
The Business of Policing

As an American citizen, you have to understand the business of policing. As much as you would like to believe that police are here to serve and protect you, there are some facts that you need to know. Policing is more aggressive in today's America than ever. This reality, according to a February 2019 article raised this concern with the headline: "The Prison Industry in the United States: Big Business or a New Form of Slavery?"

In her article, Vicky Peláez argues that the current form of aggressive policing in America is not due to a severe increase of criminal activity in the country, but rather a need to feed the prison industrial complex. She writes that prison labor has its roots in slavery, suggesting that the idea of free or cheap labor is a driving force in the mass incarceration efforts in America.

Some cities have what's called "Stop and Frisk" laws, which means that a police officer can stop any individual on the street without a suspicion of a crime, request identification, check for warrants, and frisk them for an illegal weapon. We now have video cameras at stoplights and patrol cars are equipped with license plate scanners that give a law-enforcement officer the ability to see if the vehicle is properly registered, or if the owner of the vehicle has a valid driver's license. In times past, most of this information would be gathered after someone had committed a crime or infraction that gave the officer probable cause to stop them. The law enforcement community would tell you that these are necessary precautions needed to keep you safe. These aggressive policing tactics are in direct violation of your rights. Unfortunately, Black American men bear the brunt of this aggressive form of policing and make up the majority of the incarcerated here in the United States.

Recently, a young Black man was topped and arrested by a police officer in California for eating a sandwich outside of a Bay Area Rapid Transit (BART) station. The young man bought the sandwich on the grounds, but didn't notice the "No Eating" sign posted. Although eating a sandwich was the young man's offense, the officer had a tight grip on the young man's backpack.

In her article, **Peláez** goes on to say that, after the Civil War (1861-1865), a system of "hiring out prisoners" was introduced in order to continue the slavery tradition. Freed slaves were charged with not carrying out their sharecropping commitments (cultivating someone else's land in exchange for part of the harvest) or petty thievery—which was almost never proven.

They were also "hired out" for cotton picking, working in mines, and building railroads. From 1870 until 1910 in the state of Georgia, 88% of hired-out convicts were Black. In Alabama, 93% of hired-out miners were Black. In Mississippi, a huge prison farm, similar to the old slave plantations, known as Parchman Plantation, replaced the system of hiring out convicts. It eventually closed in 1972.

To link the past to the present, **Peláez** says, "Today, a new set of markedly racist laws is imposing slave labor and sweatshops on the criminal justice system, now known as the Prison Industrial Complex." She also highlights just how serious this problem is by offering these staggering statistics: "There are approximately two million inmates in the U.S.

either in state, federal, or private prisons throughout the country. According to California Prison Focus, 'no other society in human history has imprisoned so many of its own citizens.'"

The U.S. has locked up a half million more people than China, which has a population five times greater than the U.S. The United States holds 25% of the world's prison population, but only 5% of the world's people. From less than 300,000 inmates in 1972, the jail population grew to two million by the year 2000. Ten years ago, there were only five private prisons in the country with a total population of 2,000 inmates. Now, there are one hundred prisons with 62,000 inmates. It is expected that by the coming decade, that number will hit 360,000, according to statistics.

Peláez further asserts that at least thirty-seven states have legalized the contracting of prison labor to private corporations that mount their operations inside state prisons. These companies include IBM, Boeing, Motorola, Microsoft, AT&T, Texas Instruments, Dell, Compaq, Honeywell, Hewlett-Packard, Nortel, Lucent Technologies, 3Com, Intel, Northern

Telecom, Nordstrom, Revlon, Macy's, Pierre Cardin, and Target.

Between 1980 and 1994, profits soared from $392 million to $1.31 billion. Inmates in state penitentiaries generally receive minimum wage for their work. However, in Colorado, they get about $2 per hour—well under the current federal minimum wage of $7.25 per hour. This very issue is at the heart of this huge divide between law enforcement and communities across America. The pressure to feed the beast is undoubtedly the driving force behind so many bad encounters in which citizens' rights are violated, rules are bent by law enforcement officers, and drugs are planted on the innocent to fill vacancies in private prisons. As one New York City police officer puts it, "We're stopping kids on the way to school, on the way home from school, in their stairwells all to try to get the numbers up."

Although Black Americans bear the brunt of the impact of this aggressive policing and ambition to fill private prisons as Peláez suggests, this aggressive style of policing, in many ways, is the conduit that empowers the prison industrial complex.

Chapter Four
Understanding the Encounters

There are many scenarios in which everyday citizens might find themselves in an encounter with a law enforcement officer. In this chapter, we will look at three of the most common types of encounters and learn important steps that you need to take to protect yourself. Whenever you find yourself in an encounter, you should go into the situation making two assumptions.

The first assumption is that the officer knows exactly who you are and exactly what you did. With this assumption, you must understand that every question that is asked of you is an attempt to get you to admit what you did – or what you're being suspected of doing. If you are in fact guilty of something, do not incriminate yourself. Any statement can and will be used against you in a court of law.

The second assumption is to assume that the officer doesn't have any information about you, nor does he have any reasonable articulable suspicion that you have committed a crime.

With this assumption, you must understand that every question that's asked of you is to get you to disclose to the officer information in order to charge you with a crime. A confession of guilt will undermine whatever defense that your attorney will try to make on your behalf. The first thing that you need to know when dealing with a law enforcement officer is to listen, not speak.

It's crucial that you hear what's being asked or demanded of you by the officer. Often law enforcement officers will ask you to do something in a demanding tone, or in a way that makes you believe that you have no choice in the matter. If you listen carefully, you'll be able to clearly evaluate whether or not the command is something that you're lawfully obligated to follow. For example, if an officer makes a normal traffic stop, and the driver was speeding in a vehicle with more than one occupant, and the officer requests identification from everyone in the car, you must evaluate the legality of the request. Unless you're in a Stop and Identify state, the passengers have not committed an infraction and are not required by law to produce their identification cards.

Knock at Your Door

There could be any number of reasons that a law enforcement officer might be at your front door: a complaint from a neighbor, a warrant for your arrest, an interview regarding an investigation, or service of a legal notice.

You need to remember a few things in this instance. First, don't open your door until you confirm they are at the right location and you've received the name(s) and badge number(s) of each law enforcement officer present. This is also important in order to ensure that the officers are legitimate. Believe it or not, there are many imposters.

Speak through your screen, a window, or a chained door if at all possible. Never give consent to an officer to enter or search your home for any reason unless you are presented with a warrant signed by a judge authorizing them to do so. Contrary to what some might think, it is not that easy for officers to obtain a search warrant to search your home. There must be some established form of probable cause in order to convince a judge to sign a warrant to search someone's home. If they have a warrant for the arrest of you or a family member, it does not mean that you have to allow them in your home. If the warrant is for your arrest, and they can positively confirm by picture or description that you are indeed the person that they're looking for, then it's probably in your best interest to surrender.

One tactic that may be used by officers is to bang on the door and yell the name of the Police Department or Sheriff's Office. They do this hoping that all the noise and aggression will raise your level of fear and uncertainty so high that you are willing to do anything in order to feel calm again. For the majority of us who don't usually have a lot of dealings with law enforcement at our homes, we might panic, run to the door, and open it without asking to see a warrant or getting their badge numbers and names.

If the officers say that they have a warrant to search your property, politely ask to see the warrant. Take your time and review it to make sure, first and foremost, that the warrant has your address on it, that it's to *search* your home, and that the warrant is signed by a judge. These tips are for you and your family's protection. Law enforcement exists for your protection.

There have been instances all over the country where law enforcement officers have raided the wrong house and have traumatized families, killed innocent people, and even killed pets. Police are not infallible. A data-entry mistake, a mistaken identity, a false claim, or any human error could lead to an armed law enforcement officer showing up at your home.

Not following these simple steps that most officers understand and respect can potentially be devastating to your family. In Atlanta, Georgia, in 2006, an elderly woman's home was mistakenly raided by police in search of drugs. The ninety-two-year-old woman was shot and killed by officers. Investigators determined that the raid was based on false information that stated that illegal drugs were present in the woman's house. The officers involved in this case were sentenced to five to ten years in prison.

In Detroit, Michigan, a two-year-old baby girl was burned to death while sleeping, struck by flash bombs used by law enforcement. In Chicago, Illinois, a mother and her four children were woken by screaming officers ordering them out of their house. The mother and her four children were all handcuffed for

more than thirty minutes before the officers'
mistake was discovered.

Always ask officers to review warrants.
Never allow officers in your home without
names and badge numbers. You are afforded
these rights and not making use of them could
put you and your family's safety at risk. There
are, however, exceptions to the rules. These
instances fall under what's called exigent
circumstances.

Typically, if a police officer knocks on
your door, they usually have a good reason for
doing so. What I mean by "good" is that they
usually have a lawful reason to knock on your
door. Don't open your door until you know
that they're at the right house, and you've asked
for names and badge numbers. This ensures
that these are real law enforcement officers. If
an officer shows up at your door, the first thing
that you need to know is to never open your
door to give access to you or your home until
you understand why he or she is at your door.
That means talk through a locked screen door, a
chained door, or a window. If you give consent
to enter your home if he or she sees or smells
anything illegal you can be charged with a
crime. There have been many instances where

unsuspecting citizens have opened their door and officers stuck a foot in the door and prevented them from closing their own door. Once you've taken this simple step to protect yourself from an unlawful entry or access to your home, politely ask the officer for their names and badge numbers and offer your assistance. If there is a warrant for your arrest, or for anyone that lives in your home, then the warrant should be displayed for you to read. Remember a warrant for someone's arrest is not a warrant to search your home. However if you give consent to enter your home or if they physically see the person that they're looking for enter your home, they can and will enter into your home, bedroom, bathroom, or wherever. The legal term for this warrantless entry of your home is "exigent circumstances." Exigent circumstances are situations when the need of a police officer to enter or search a dwelling overrides the constitutional right to be free from warrantless searches. From the Supreme Court Ruling in the case of *People v. Riddle (1978),* it is explained that, "When emergency circumstances exist… constitutional requirements, such as the need for a warrant… may be excused because of overriding necessity." All states have provisions that allow a warrantless search in exigent circumstances. Courts have struggled over the years to clearly define these circumstances. Whether a situation constitutes exigent circumstances or not will typically be determined by the judge in a criminal case. Circumstances that might fall under this provision vary. For example, an officer engaged in a foot chase with a suspect believed to have snatched a purse who sees the suspect with the purse in hand enter into a residence, may enter the residence to make the arrest. Another scenario could involve a domestic violence complaint received by a resident. Upon arrival, if an officer hears someone screaming for help and no one comes to the door he will reasonably believe that someone's life might be in danger. In this situation a warrantless entry might save a life.

When police act without a warrant, it is up to them to prove that they acted appropriately. Anyone who believes his constitutional rights were violated by a warrantless entry or search should consult with an experienced criminal defense attorney for information on having the evidence suppressed.

An attorney can help to disprove a law enforcement claim of exigent circumstances in order to have illegally collected evidence kept out of the trial.

Traffic Stop

The traffic stop is probably the most common of all police encounters. The majority of people driving on the streets of America understand and accept that they're expected to have a current driver's license with them. There are, however, members of our society who challenge the legality of this requirement. While driving, you might find yourself committing some form of traffic infraction (not fully stopping at a stop sign, blocking an intersection, not signaling before turning, etc.). If a law enforcement officer believes that you have violated a traffic law, then they have the authority to stop your vehicle.

You may or may not agree with the officer's claim that you violated some traffic infraction, but if the officer pulls you over, you are required by law to present your license, registration, and proof of insurance. Upon reaching your window to discuss your infraction, the officer typically will tell you immediately who they are, what police department they represent, and why you're being stopped. After introducing themselves, the next step is to request your relevant information. While you're getting your info, the officer looks into your vehicle for anything that could be used to turn this routine traffic stop into a criminal investigation. You might think that the officer is being nice and courteous with you, but every question that's asked of you is a part of their plain-view observation of you and your vehicle. This consists of smelling your air, looking at your pockets for bulges, monitoring your speech for slurred words, or just checking to see how uncomfortable their presence makes you. For example, the officer may ask you where you're headed. This seemingly innocent question is designed to establish some kind of story that you are immediately locked into. Each question tests your knowledge of the law and of your rights. A follow-up question is typically about where you're coming from. Upon answering these questions, you are inadvertently assisting the officer in an investigation that could possibly lead to incarceration.

Innocent people don't mind answering these questions and see them as harmless. However, you have the right to not answer those questions. If you've been stopped because you drive a car that matches the description of one involved in a recent robbery at the Wal-Mart on Freedom Parkway and you tell the officer that's where you're coming from, you've placed yourself at the scene of a crime you know nothing about. Sure, this could easily be cleared up by simply bringing someone from the Wal-Mart to confirm that you're not involved. However, what if someone is adamant that it was you, or someone with you?

The number one rule for all police encounters is to get it over with as quickly as possible. The less you say, the faster the encounter will be over. Even officers who are part of the honorable majority are trained to follow a protocol that will always help them find ways to get you to admit some type of wrongdoing or to share information that can and will be used against you, so be careful. Another investigative question often asked is about the speed with which you were driving. An unsuspecting motorist might admit to not knowing their speed and being in a hurry. The best way to avoid prolonging the stop or potentially getting yourself into trouble by talking too much is to respectfully say that you do not wish to engage in conversation about your personal life. Once you've made this statement you have just asserted your Fifth Amendment right.

One final question worth highlighting is the last question often asked as the officer prepares to process your information. Just as they get ready to walk away, they may inquire if you have any drugs, guns, knives, hand grenades, or even a bazooka in the vehicle! The one thing that you need to understand about this question is that everything that was just mentioned is illegal, except guns and knives unless you're a convicted felon or on probation or parole. So, the question boxes an unsuspecting motorist into a whole set of new questions such as where is the gun located? Is the gun registered to you? Can you step out of your vehicle for me?

Many people don't understand that the officer has the right to ask you to step out of the vehicle and refuse to do so, not knowing that this could possibly escalate this situation. At this point, the officer can legally break your window and even use physical force to remove you from your vehicle. For the officer's safety, the Supreme Court has given officers the right to ask the driver of the vehicle to step out if there is the potential for the officer to be hurt. There is no argument for this. However, for *your* safety, be sure to ask the officer to call a supervisor to the scene.

If you're recording, when the supervisor arrives, ask them both exactly what you did to make the officer feel unsafe "so I won't make that mistake again." The reason for this question is to hear on camera what made the officer pull you out of the car, just in case this stop ends up in court for any reason. Remember, your goal now is to protect yourself during an encounter. This is essential, because, more than likely, the law enforcement officer will return to your vehicle to retrieve your firearm whether you legally have a right to carry it or not. When this request is made, in the process of complying, say to the officer, "I know that you have the right to ask me to step out of the vehicle, however, be advised that I do not consent to any searches of my person, property or documents." We've already covered the officer's right to pat you down for weapons, so expect a pat down.

If you are a passenger in the car, you may be asked to identify yourself as well. Once again, depending on state laws, you may or may not be required to identify yourself or engage in any conversation. If you choose this route, simply say to the officer "I do not wish to engage in any conversation with you." Do not answer any questions after that point.

Before the officer gets to your vehicle, lock your doors, put your windows up with the exception of the driver window and raise it to a little above halfway. No matter what is said, no law requires you to let any other windows down, or that you let your driver's window down any more than enough to clearly communicate with the officer. Remember, you want to keep this encounter as brief as possible, so keep your required documents readily available.

Consensual Contact
Consensual contact is a tactic used by police to stop and question you without reasonable articulable suspicion or probable cause with a hope to find some reason to detain

you or arrest you. A police officer may approach you in public, looking to establish consensual contact with you for the sole purpose of conducting a non-threatening, non-aggressive investigation. During small talk, he is conducting a plain-view observation of you. The goal is to find something that can be used as reasonable articulable suspicion or probable cause to legally detain you, or, at the very least, run your name and birthdate through the database in search of outstanding warrants.

A legal detainment is one step away from an arrest. You are not required by law to have a consensual conversation with the police. If approached while walking down the street, for instance, slow down just a little to show respect but continue to walk until the officer either verbally or physically demands that you stop. You may simply say, "I do not wish to engage in 'consensual conversation' with you. Have a nice day."

If an officer does demand you to stop, you are not free to leave. This becomes a *lawful detainment*. A lawful detainment means that the officer has a reasonable suspicion that you have committed a crime, are about to commit a crime, or you're in the act of committing a crime. If the officer cannot give you a specific crime that he suspects you of committing, then there is a good chance that this is an unlawful detainment. In order to legally detain you, they must have reasonable articulable suspicion.

In order to determine what their suspicions are, you must ask, "Am I free to go?" If they say anything other than "yes," then you are being detained. If not, take that as a no and continue on your way. If they don't already have a reason to detain you, don't wait around for them to find or create one. If the officer says "Yes, you are being detained," then stop and ask "What crime do you suspect me of?" Often, citizens are stopped, questioned, searched, and identified without knowing why they were stopped. Remember, he needs a reasonable, articulable suspicion that you have committed a crime in order for it to be a legal detainment.

If there is a crime that he or she suspects you of committing, then the officer will readily disclose that information to you. If not, then he'll give you a generic answer to the question, such as, "That's what we're trying to figure out," or "I'm just talking to you." That means he is looking for a reason to arrest you. Your next question should be to ask if you are free to go. If the answer is "yes," then immediately walk away. If the answer is "no," you're not free to go. Your next words should be, "I wish to remain silent until I'm free to go." Generally, the next move that the officer will make is to ask for your identification card. Remember, unless you're in a Stop and Identify state, you are not required by law to say or give any information unless you have been lawfully arrested. Remain quiet unless you're asking "Am I free to go?"

The goal for you is to do what you can to make any encounter as brief as possible. So, unless you know this officer personally, feel comfortable, and would love to chat it up with them, stick to the guidelines I've outlined in this chapter.

Chapter Five
The Escalation

When an officer engaging in questionable actions takes issue with you asserting your rights, he or she might use several intimidation tactics in order to bring you to a state of submission and cooperation. These tactics are designed to subconsciously take your freedom in hopes that the rest of you will follow. It can be extremely scary.

The first step typically is the use of a more intimidating tone, indicating that the officer is becoming agitated with you asserting your rights. During the escalation, it's not uncommon to hear profanity in an aggressive tone. If the officer knows that they have no legal basis to demand your information, they will ask you for your identification in a demanding tone. It's important that you pay attention so that you can ensure you hear the question or the demand. Just because an officer uses an aggressive tone and profanity does not mean that you have to answer the question, or that the command is lawful.

You should know that asserting your rights as a citizen of this country is in no way an obstruction of justice. However, if you don't understand what's happening, the threat of arrest can cause anxiety and confusion. You'll have to ask yourself if your freedom is worth pushing down your nervousness and fear so that you can think clearly and choose the best behavior in that moment. It's imperative for you to study the terms covered in chapter two and understand them well. Knowing them with certainty will help you to approach your encounter from a position of knowledge.

Intimidation tactics are designed to make you think and feel as if you've done something wrong, or worse, committed a crime. During the escalation you must constantly remind yourself that you haven't done anything wrong. If they had anything on you, you would be under arrest.

If the threat of arrest does not frighten you into compliance, you may be asked to turn around and put your hands behind your back. You will likely be informed that you're going to be detained until more information is presented. This is definitely a pressure point for many of us because this is serious business.

A common mistake that people make during the escalation is that, because you know that you have not committed a crime and the officer has no lawful reason to detain you, you start to resist and tell the officer that they can't hold you. It may not be lawful for the officer to do whatever they want, but don't get verbally aggressive or resist being cuffed. An inadvertent touch, bump, or push of the officer could lead to a charge of assault on a police officer.

Cuffing you is a tactic, just like having an aggressive tone. If you are being cuffed for an investigatory detainment, don't lose your composure. If you haven't committed a crime before your detainment, be careful not to commit a crime during or after your detainment. You can expect a pat down at this point if they haven't already done so. Immediately inform the officer that you do not consent to any searches or seizures of your personal property or documents. If you know of any statutes in connection to anything that's said or done to you during this escalation, respectfully make the officers aware of the fact. This will help you if this encounter leads to your arrest.

One other tactic that might be used is the officer claiming that they smell alcohol. Naturally you may be asked if you had anything to drink. If you say you have, the next question is often about the amount you consumed. The officer may mention a strong smell of alcohol. At this point, whether you are intoxicated or not, the officer will generally insist you step outside of the vehicle to possibly administer some type of sobriety exercises. Or they may state that they smell marijuana and would like to run the K-9 around your vehicle for a free air sniff. You'll be asked to step out of the vehicle. If the officer smelled it, the K-9 Unit will. Always be mindful of the time that your encounter begins and what time it ends. A typical traffic stop should last approximately twenty to thirty minutes. Anything longer than that can be scrutinized in a court of law. Both of these instances are a clear indicator as to why you should keep your windows up, and your driver's side window should be down no more than enough to clearly communicate with the officer.

When given the opportunity to speak, politely express to the officer that you do not consent to the search or seizure of your person, property, or documents. Also express that you want to make sure that the officer's body cam is on and that it remains on for the entire time they are on the scene. Request that they do not turn off, mute, or cover the body cam as you interact. Audio and video captured on a body cam is evidence and any attempt to tamper with evidence is a crime and could lead to the officer's termination, arrest, and even conviction of a felony for tampering with evidence or obstructing justice.

This stop is now a criminal investigation of you and your vehicle. Ask the K-9 officer for the name and badge number of the K-9 that will be conducting the free air sniff around your vehicle. The answers are important for your protection. Ask the officer how the K-9 will alert them to the smell of marijuana. Will the K-9 sit, scratch, bark, etc.? This simply gives you the opportunity to know if the K-9 actually gives an alert or not as well as documents the officer's answer. Inquire about how the K-9, if he does alert, would know whether or not the smell is coming from around your vehicle, or if you stopped where someone dumped an ashtray on the side of the road, or if a vehicle that just drove past has the smell of marijuana coming from it.

Finally, ask the officer if the K-9 has ever given a false alert. Assuming that the officer hangs around this long, inform the officer that you are aware of his right to conduct a free air sniff around your vehicle, however, you do not give the officer permission to touch your vehicle, nor do you give the K-9 the permission to touch your vehicle.

You, nor a jury that may have to decide whether or not your rights were violated, have no way of knowing whether the officer has touched a bag of marijuana before entering your vehicle and planted the scent on your vehicle or not. Request that the officer doesn't give the K-9 any commands during the free air sniff as neither you nor a jury can know exactly what the officer's commands mean.

If the smell of marijuana is anywhere near your vehicle that the officer smelled at your window, without question, the K-9 will smell it immediately. If there is an alert, be sure that you note where the K-9 alerted. If you're not certain, be sure to ask the K-9 officer where the K-9 alerted on your vehicle for your records.

By exercising your rights, you ultimately prevent an illegal search and seizure of your property. At every chance you get, be sure to ask if you are free to go. By this point, if the officer has nothing else to do, you be free to go. Searching for some reason to arrest you – not because they believe that you are a criminal or have committed a crime, but because you had the audacity to stand up for yourself and not allow your rights to be violated – is an infringement on your freedom.

Chapter Six
Officer Conduct

A 2019 *USA Today* article by John Kelley and Mark Nichols highlights a set of alarming facts about law enforcement practices when it comes to the discipline and removal of bad law enforcement officers. The study revealed that many officers who have engaged in crimes, such as domestic violence, theft, falsifying documents, sexual assaults, false arrest, police brutality, drug dealing, abuse of power, perjury, and even murder, are rarely punished.

One of the most disturbing claims in the article was that much of the misbehavior, including criminal acts done by law enforcement officers, is deliberately kept from the public and, in some cases, has been removed from the officer's record completely. Bad cops often remain on the job without the fear of losing credentials, rank, or future promotions.

The article analyzed disciplinary records from hundreds of departments and state licensing boards in nearly every state in the country. For the first time, there is a list of more than 30,000 law enforcement officers who have been decertified (stripped of their credentials to serve as a law enforcement officer). Officers with records of misconduct typically try to hide in small towns with less oversight in hopes that their atrocious conduct and criminal activity will be overlooked. At least eight law enforcement officers became police chiefs after having been previously found guilty of a crime.

Jeronimo Yanez, the officer who shot and killed motorist Philando Castile, had previous documentation of misconduct in his file. Castile, who attempted to get away from the stop, was unarmed. Yanez claimed that he was in fear for his life when he fired several shots into the vehicle, killing Castile. Janez avoided conviction. However, a video surfaced later in which this officer stopped two young men that he suspected of a hit and run. In the video, viewers can see and hear Yanez's aggressive style of policing, demanding that the passenger of the vehicle show his identification. The kid refused because he knew his rights and requested a supervisor to come onto the scene. Upon the supervisor's arrival, the young men were released. If law-abiding citizens can be harmed by a non-compliant officer who has no respect for the law, that officer has no business working in law enforcement. The troubling reality is that some members of our law enforcement have received a felony conviction. Convicted felons are not allowed to carry firearms or work as law enforcement officers in the United States.

A police officer who had been fired for committing a felony, and again for perjury, became the police chief of Amsterdam, Ohio, a small struggling steel town in the hills of west Pittsburg. In all, the study identified more than thirty other chiefs and sheriffs with questionable pasts. One chief in Arkansas landed a job even though city officials knew that he had crashed his car into a house, then falsely reported that it had been stolen. The chief of Kansas College's police force had been charged with a felony years earlier for dragging a man out of his car at gunpoint. With this type of oversight, or lack thereof, in the law enforcement community, how can we trust that a law enforcement officer we come in contact with on the street is an honorable professional who takes his job to protect and serve seriously? Overall, the study found that of the

750,000 police officers and agencies around the country, up to 88,000 officers have been accused, charged, and convicted while others continue to patrol the streets of the United States.

Chapter Seven
The 3 C's

The 3 C's are Cover Yourself, Calm Down, and Comply. These represent the three major steps that you need to take during an encounter with a law enforcement officer. These measures will undoubtedly help you protect yourself.

Cover Yourself

Covering yourself means being prepared for an encounter. Understanding the current aggressive style of policing taking place in America, it is in your best interest to prepare yourself for an encounter. The best way to cover yourself is to abide by the law. If you don't agree with the seat-belt law, breaking the law is not the most intelligent way to protest it. If the law is on the books, you must obey it. A broken law, or traffic violation, is all the probable cause needed to legally stop, detain, and possibly arrest you depending on the nature of the offense.

Knowing and being willing to assert your basic rights is a critical step in covering yourself during an encounter. Remember the Miranda Rights:

- You have the right to remain silent. Anything you say can be used against you in court.
- You have the right to consult a lawyer before answering any questions.
- You have the right to have a lawyer during questions.
- If you cannot afford a lawyer, one will be appointed for you.
- You have the right to have a lawyer during questioning.
- You have the right to stop answering at any time.

Also recall these key parts of the Fifth Amendment:

- Right to a fair and speedy trial by jury.
- Double Jeopardy (you cannot be tried for the same crime twice).
- Due process of the law.

According to a recent study done by the Innocence Project, 25% of wrongful convictions were overturned by use of newly discovered DNA evidence. It has been asserted that defendants made false confessions, admissions, or statements to law enforcement officers due to real or perceived intimidation by law enforcement, exhaustion, stress, hunger, or mental limitations.

You must cover yourself by limiting your conversation with police officers.

It is equally important when it comes to covering yourself that you record the encounter. The Constitution of The United States gives United States citizens the right to record police officers or any other government officials during the course of their duties. Police have been known to tell citizens to stop recording and threaten them with arrest in order to intimidate them.

Until the officer takes your phone or camera by force, continue recording through the threats. The officer is either ill-informed or is knowingly trying to deprive you of a constitutionally protected activity. As a citizen of the United States of America, you have the right to use this tool to protect yourself during an encounter.

As persistent as the officer is, you must match that persistence with your knowledge and confidence of your right to do so. Citizens all over the country are recording their encounters and have had charges dropped due to the video evidence provided from a cell phone or camera video.

Look into purchasing your own body cam so that you don't have to hold a phone or camera in your hands. Officers often claim that for their safety they don't want anything in your hands that they can mistake for a weapon.

Take this seriously. Knowing and exercising your right to produce evidence of what actually happened, what you said and did, as well as what was said by the officer or officers, can make a great difference in your favor if charges are brought against you. An officer may also try to convince you that he is recording so you don't need to. Unfortunately, body cam footage of encounters with officers has been damaged or gone missing in the past. You are responsible for your own safety and for evidence of what occurred.

Feel free to request the officer to turn his body cam on. Record the encounter until the officer lawfully dispossesses you of your own recording device.

According to the American Civil Liberties Union (ACLU) website:

- *Taking photographs of things that are plainly visible from public spaces is a constitutional right and that includes federal buildings, transportation facilities, and police and other government officials carrying out their duties. Unfortunately, there is a widespread, continuing pattern of law enforcement officers ordering people to stop taking photographs from public places, and harassing, detaining and arresting those who fail to comply.*

- *When in public spaces where you are lawfully present, you have the right to photograph anything that is in plain view.*

- *When you are on private property, the property owner may set rules about the taking of photographs.*

- *Police officers may not confiscate or demand to view your digital photographs or video without a warrant.*

- *Police may not delete your photographs or video under any circumstances.*

- *Police officers may legitimately order citizens to cease activities that are truly interfering with legitimate law enforcement operations.*
- *Note that the right to photograph does not give you a right to break any other laws.*

Calm Down

Calming yourself down means keeping a level head during the law enforcement contact. Studies have shown that most people experience a significantly heightened neurological reaction in high-stress situations. In this heightened state, people have been known to make decisions that they normally would not. It's not uncommon under certain circumstances, such as a police encounter, for a person to experience some type of panic attack, lose the ability to focus, or struggle to recall certain familiar information.

Another reaction that people have during a high-stress situation is that of anger. Uncontrolled anger does not adhere to the rules of survival. It takes one into a full-blown "fight or flight" state of mind. It denies you the ability to think about the potential consequences of your actions. Anger seeks immediate vindication. A mere accusation made against some people sends them into a total and complete state of uncontrollable anger. Uncontrolled anger can be particularly dangerous during an encounter with a law enforcement officer.

Citizens are about nine times more likely to be hurt, harmed, or even killed during an encounter with a law enforcement officer than the officer. Every word that's uttered from your mouth, your body language, the movement of your hands, and the tone of your voice can be like dumping gasoline on a fire.

In a 2014 case, a New York man named Eric Garner was approached by several NYPD officers who believed that he was breaking the law by selling loose cigarettes on a street corner. When approached by the officers, Mr. Garner argued that he was not committing a crime and that he was being harassed by the officers. During his protest of their claim, he avoided being cuffed and blocked officers from grabbing him in their effort to arrest him. Ultimately, he was placed in an illegal chokehold and killed by NYPD officer Daniel Pantaleo, who was ultimately fired as a result of his actions. It doesn't matter how small you think the stop is. It can escalate quickly if you don't remain calm and control your words, movement, and actions. Don't become hostile or belligerent. That will work against you during the encounter and in a court of law.

Given the fact that you're not sure why an officer is making contact with you, you will be a little rattled by the situation. If you've done something wrong and the officer sees you, expect the contact. Remember, if you haven't committed a crime, then the law is on your side. If you are uncomfortable and decide to run from an officer, you've created a reasonable articulable suspicion, which now gives him the right to legally detain you, pat you down, and question you.

You are still under no obligation to say anything. He or she still has to have probable cause to arrest you. They may even throw the charge of resisting by flight out there to intimidate you in hopes that you will be willing to cooperate with them as they start the process of investigating you. However, in order for the charge of resisting by flight to hold up in a court of law, it must have been made clear to you that you were under arrest before you ran.

If you hear this charge and you were not placed under arrest before you ran, then tell the officer you were resisting unwanted contact. This exchange should solicit a response from the officer. You should be recording if possible. If not, his body cam may pick up his response.

<u>There are three questions that you should ask in any encounter:</u>

- **Am I under arrest?** It's essential that you get as much information from the officer as you can. This is the most important question of the encounter.

- **Am I being detained?** This question should provoke the officer to tell you what he or she wants with you. The officer must have reasonable articulable suspicion in order to legally detain you.

- **Am I free to go?** You've asked if you're under arrest and you've asked if you're being detained. If you have not received an affirmative response, then ask if you are free to go.

Chapter Eight
Comply

An encounter with law enforcement can be dangerous and every threat made to you, lawful or unlawful, can quickly become a reality. Even if you're absolutely positive that you have done nothing wrong and you have your video to prove it, there is a real chance that you can be unlawfully arrested. In the event that you are placed under arrest, don't resist, don't fight, and don't become belligerent. Simply comply with the officer's request to put your hands behind your back. Your compliance with the officer's orders will hopefully prevent you from being harmed by an officer. Your compliance robs them of what they desperately need – some kind of charge to justify your arrest.

If you know that the order is not lawful, inform the officer that your compliance to the order is due to a fear of arrest or potential harm to you or others present. Complying under duress establishes the fact that you are aware that your rights are being violated and that you intend to file a formal complaint with the department. If you have taken the appropriate steps to protect yourself, you have video and audio evidence that will support your complaint and aid in your defense.

Complying with an officer's orders does not mean that you are participating in the violation of your rights. The truth is that the law is in control of the encounter. The officer is hired by the people to enforce the laws that have already been established by legislators who we vote into office. Before you or the officer ever meet, the law was already established around the encounter. It is vital that you take the time to learn the laws regarding law enforcement and follow them as closely as possible.

In the event that you encounter a law enforcement officer, there are clearly established laws that outline what you can do legally during the encounter—that is, what is legally required of you and what is legally acceptable of the officer. Remember, if the officer demands that you stop and speak with him, the law is clearly established that he or she needs a reasonable articulable suspicion that you have either committed a crime, are about to commit a crime, or that you're in the act of

committing a crime. If they cannot articulate
the crime they reasonably believed that you
have committed, then the law says that the stop
or detainment is unlawful. On the other hand, if
the officer can articulate a reasonable suspicion
that you have committed a crime, then he or she
can lawfully detain you to investigate their
suspicion. The law also has clearly established
that you don't legally have to answer any
questions that she might ask without a lawyer
or legal counsel.

Chapter Nine
Resisting Arrest

Resisting arrest can often lead to an additional charge when a person verbally or physically resists an officer who has informed them that they are under arrest. Never attempt to resist an officer who has placed you under arrest. The fact that you disagree with the charge or the officer's attitude is not important at this point. Resisting arrest can lead to you being seriously hurt. Officers will use whatever level of force they deem necessary to bring a suspect under control. There is, however, a way to legally resist your arrest and not accrue any additional charges in the process.

Many unsuspecting citizens find themselves facing this charge because they wholeheartedly believe that the officer is in error, and that they have not done anything to be arrested. The only thing that matters during the encounter is being safe and unharmed. If the officer has placed you under arrest, trust the process and don't make things worse for yourself. If the officer is in error, you will have your day in court to fight and prove your innocence. If you have taken the appropriate steps to cover yourself, the proof of what you did is at your fingertips. Upon your release, find an attorney who will take your case and use the evidence you gathered to make your case against the word of the officer.

When You Are Arrested (Unlawfully)

The biggest challenge in defending yourself, as a citizen, is finding the money to pay for a lawyer to defend you in a court of law. If finances are an issue, you can contact entities such as the American Civil Liberties Union (A.C.L.U.) or the National Association for the Advancement of Colored People (NAACP) — civil advocacy groups that can be helpful in matters such as these. File an official complaint with the police department that the officer is a representative of.

Filing the complaint will at the very least make the department aware of the officer's conduct and establish a paper trail. Going online and getting as much information as you can before you actually go in to file the complaint will hopefully tell you what steps you need to take, who you need to speak with, and where you need to go.

Go online and read the policy on filing a complaint against the officer. After you have taken the time to read the policy online, call the department with any additional questions that you might have about filing a complaint. Record your conversation and ask for the name of the person that you are speaking with and the badge number of the officer. If your state requires that you inform a second party that you're recording your phone conversation, you must make it clear that you are recording the conversation.

Protect yourself. Go into the police station with your camera recording and ask for a complaint form or for information on how to file an official complaint against an officer. You have every right to record a law enforcement officer in the lobby of the police station that is open to the public. Many of the same tactics that were discussed earlier might be used to try and intimidate you to stop recording, or even to not file the complaint, so stick closely to The 3 C's in order to protect yourself. After filing your official complaint, ask how long it should take for you to hear back from someone. Hopefully, you have an attorney who will walk you through this process. However, you should be able to take care of most of this on your own.

You also need to make a Freedom of Information Act, or FOIA request. This gives everyday citizens the right to go into the public records department of the police station and request the body cam and dash cam footage of every officer that was present during your encounter. There will be a charge for copies but nothing too significant. If you're trying to handle this case on your own, you will have the option to take this information into court with you to help in your defense.

Don't get frustrated by how long this might take. You must be prepared for the long ride of resisting your arrest. Set a schedule for yourself to follow up on your complaint and document every contact that you make, so that you never have to rely on memory to explain who you spoke with, what day and time you spoke to them, if you went in person or called, and what was said during that exchange.

It might take years, but you must remain patient and diligent in your quest to resist your arrest. It may have happened three years ago, but the facts surrounding your encounter remain the same. You should have the encounter documented from start to finish including statements that were made by officers, actions that were taken by officers, and everything needed to help an attorney better represent you. A typical and predictable stalling of the process is designed to hold you off until you get tired of calling and getting the run around and you become so frustrated with the process that you give up and let your false arrest stand.

Don't become so consumed with this that it prevents you from moving forward with your life. Continue to live your life to the best of your ability while you're waiting on your day in court to clear your good name and succeed at resisting your arrest. The final step that you need to take is to file a civil lawsuit against the department, the city, and every entity that needs to be held accountable in your case.

Video and Audio Evidence Matters

One case that has been in the news is the 2017 case in which a young man by the name of Henry Newson was attacked and falsely arrested by Fort Worth police officer Jon

Romer. Romer punched Newson and wrestled him to the ground as Newson, who had been discharged from the hospital, was in the lobby waiting for his mom to pick him up. He was being questioned by a security guard while he was using a bystander's cellphone to call his mom. Officer Romer approached the three men and began to question Mr. Newson and ended up punching him several times, wrestling him to the ground, and eventually arresting him for resisting arrest and trespassing. After the video surfaced, Officer Romer was charged with lying to the grand jury, because he said that he told Mr. Newson before he punched him that he was under arrest, a claim that the video contradicted and led to him being fired and convicted.

Three and a half years later, Mr. Newson got his day in court and successfully resisted his arrest and the officer was convicted. Newson filed a civil suit against the hospital, the police department, and the city of Fort Worth. If you take the practice of protecting yourself seriously, you can legally and lawfully resist your arrest.

Seventeen-year-old Laquan McDonald was shot and killed by Chicago police officer,

Jason Van Dyke. Police initially reported that the teen behaved erratically as he walked down the street, refused to put down the knife he carried, and lunged at them. Preliminary reports described the incident similarly and ruled the shooting justified. Van Dyke was not charged in the shooting at that time. A court would later order that the dash-cam video taken from the officer's vehicle be released. It revealed that McDonald was actually walking away from the police when he was shot. Officer Van Dyke was arrested the same day that the video was released and charged with first-degree murder. He was later convicted of second-degree murder, as well as sixteen counts of aggravated battery for the sixteen shots fired into the teen's body.

Conclusion

The wrong thing to do is to hold the entire law enforcement community responsible for the actions of a few. Some arguments have been made that police departments willingly cover for this type of behavior. However, keep in mind that in most cases, the chief or captain was not on the scene. These officials typically trust that the information that was received is true and factual. When the city receives information from video and audio recordings contradicting an initial report, they usually reach a different conclusion.

Don't consider it disrespectful to take these necessary steps to protect yourself during an encounter with law enforcement. Think of your family and friends, your career, and all the parts of your life that can be negatively affected by an encounter with a law enforcement officer. It's not being disrespectful. It's being free.

Sources

1. https://www.usa.gov/history
2. https://www.archives.gov/founding-docs/constitution-transcript
3. https://www.archives.gov/founding-docs/bill-of-rights-transcript
4. https://www.washingtonpost.com/news/true-crime/wp/2016/06/22/study-finds-1100-police-officers-per-year-or-3-per-day-are-arrested-nationwide/
5. https://www.uscourts.gov/about-federal-courts/types-cases/criminal-cases